everything
and nothing

E.S. Higgins

E.S. Higgins Copyright © 2026 Peanut Prints

All rights reserved.

ISBN: 978-0-6485460-9-2

PEANUT PRINTS

Preface

The feeling of *being* is indescribable, and all the words in this book fall hopelessly short. These poems are an attempt, at best, to describe the torrent of daily life and how we can feel as individuals trying to find a place in the world. You are everything and nothing at all. Before you there's a beach, ready for you to leave your tracks in the sand. But, the second you take a step, your marks are washed away by the sea. So that the only time you really exist is right now, in this moment, where your feet are.

So much of life is an absurdity, a collective belief that places importance on things that are unimportant in matters of the soul and the universe. It's easy to lose yourself in them and forget the things that really mean something to you. Who you are, and where you're going, the world as you see it, and the beauty of everyday experiences that we overlook when we lose ourselves in the rush and routine of daily life.

These poems are my unqualified way of trying to express the feeling of being everything and nothing all at once, in a world that needs you to exist.

I hope you enjoy.

on life

**You are everything
and nothing at all**

  When you feel as if you don't belong
Or that the world would be better off without you
You don't realise how much you are needed
Nothing exists without you
The stars, the sun and the moon
Need you to see their light
Without you
They would disappear into the night

The waves need you
To listen to how they break
The rain and the storms
Need you so you can taste
The sweetness in the air
Just before lightning strikes
None of this would matter
Without you and your life

The wind needs you
So that it can play with your hair
The earth, the rivers, the mountains
All of them need you there
They're all performing

So that they can experience what it means to be alive
Without you
None of them could share their light

You are everything
And also, nothing at all
Just a figure passing by
Catching the rain when it falls
But that's what makes life beautiful
Even though we die at the end
To witness and experience
Things that may never be again
Without you.

Take yourself seriously
if you're serious about something

I've been writing for 10 years
But I've never called myself a writer
Because I was afraid that if I took myself seriously
I'd leave myself vulnerable to judgement
To the possibility of someone disagreeing with me
And worse, that they'd be right…
So, I acted cool and casual
But on the inside, I was terrified
I wonder what might happen
If we all lay down our cards
I think that we would come to the same conclusion
We do every time
That we are all human
And imperfect
Likely to be judged
And even likelier to be disagreed with
Whether you take yourself seriously or not
So, why not take yourself seriously?
If you're serious about something
And give it everything you have
Even if it may promise nothing
But enjoyment and fulfilment
Which are the most important things of all
I know I'll write forever
Regardless of what I'm called.

The music of life

The music of life is in
the wind and how
it blows, the breaking
of waves, the falling of rain
and snow, birds calling,
Children laughing while
they play, bus engines grinding,
Cars driving past with music
Playing, pedestrian crossings,
Ringing, disrupting the silence
of night, swallowed by the endless
noise of day. The music
of life, plays when you're trying
to sleep as countless seconds
go by, drenched in silence
When you're alone at night.

**The world is a
waiting room**

The world is a waiting room
Full of people holding hands
Letting go one by one
Even though no one really understands
Why we come
Only to go
How to stop time
Or make it slow

Just for a moment
So, we can let it all sink in
One last hug, one last kiss
One last laugh, even though the time
for laughter is gone
One last sunset, one last storm
One last chance
For the wind to play with your hair
For the light to dance on the water
For one last breath of fresh air
For joy to come again
For the love and the tears
Those aching moments
When we are free from fear

One more moment
Before you let go

And pass through the door
Of the waiting room.

CYCLE

The tree fell
And lay like a corpse
Under silent bodies
That grew further away
Blocking out the sunlight
Falling leaves
Covered it until
It was finally claimed
Again.

A hungry city

The world is split equally
By those who give
And those who take
That's how it finds the balance to stay afloat

In a city full of people
Eating and being eaten all at once
To the backdrop of footsteps
Marching across the path
Some people
Think that the whole world is looking at them
But in reality, it's looking back
All around
Are the sounds of movement
And the smell of perfume and hair gel
Of sweat and dirt and grime
We are all just faces
Passing each other by
Going someplace

Construction workers are talking, laying
on some steps
Drinking coffee and smoking cigarettes
The office workers are at cafés and restaurants on chairs
There are homeless people there too but no one cares
We could just as easily be any of them

I take the place of my dad
Holding the tools of progression
That get passed down from hand to hand
A rusty shovel and a pickaxe

I get to work and start digging
Slowly burying myself beneath the sky scrapers
That are like glass colosseums
Where everyone fights to live
Only to die a thousand times by the end
of it all
Buried under stone and rubble
Packed down by the ceaseless drum of footsteps
On weekends
I drink and smoke
Just to forget a little while.

moment

  My best ideas
Are always realised in the moment
When I don't have anything to write
them down
Sometimes it feels like I spend half my life trying to
remember
The feeling of glory that passes when you least expect it.

Every day

You could walk past the same thing
Every day
And look at it differently
The feeling
Of being stuck in life
Isn't just physical
But mental and emotional

> When you're constantly focused
> On the bigger picture
> Your progress looks like
> It's standing still
> Even though
> You are moving always

If you look closer
We are all hurdling forwards
Through time
Milliseconds
Fly by in a blur

> Look around at your world
> The one you see every day
> And try to see it as though
> It's the first time
> Nothing stays the same
> Not even you

Allow yourself to change
With the world
And exist
In constant creation and recreation
Of who you are
And where you are going

                                              And above all
                                              If nothing else
                                              Be grateful
                                              For everything.

Life has to consume itself in order to survive.

YOUNG

When I was young
I stared out the window a lot
daydreaming.

AND OLD

Now that I'm older
A daydream last weeks
Sometimes months
And when I come to
From time to time
I remember that I'm alive
And there's no time to waste.

Witness

   When you are alone
You see the world for what it really is
In those glorious moments without words
A passing clarity
When everything suddenly makes sense
Now that you're unstuck from it all
For just a moment
You are an observer
The beauty in life is to be its witness
The sorrow comes when you forget that you are a part of it all
The collective movement of life
That stands still when you look for too long.

YOUTH

Underage parties, where
somehow, everyone had drinks
Doing ecstasy
At the age of sixteen
Jumping fences
An army of little shits
Dissolve into the night
Boy's going after chicks
Like badges of honour
That's just how it goes
Burn a plastic bottle
And chop off the end
of a garden hose
Tell your mum you're out doing drugs
That's what I used to do
Make it so obvious
That she doesn't believe you
Go and have fun
Just don't get caught
That's the point of being young;
To learn from it all.

Heaven and hell are the same place; it all depends on who's looking.

JUDGE

I don't know you, really
I don't know what you're going through
or how you feel
I'm limited by my bias
That can only see you in one dimension
So, you'll have to forgive my judgement
As not something to oppose who you are
But who you're perceived to be.

As the sun set it was as if someone had suddenly pulled a plug and drained all the colour from the world.

The only people who make light of death
Are the ones who are terrified to die.

Evolve

We will wipe ourselves into
extinction
Not through war
But by loss of ethics
When we lose touch of our humanity
And become machine.

**The sweetest things in life
are ordinary**

  The greatest mistake he ever made
Was expecting life to be extraordinary
He missed the whole point,
the importance of learning to find
wonder
In what is ordinary
The things that happen every day
Love, marriage and kids
Small conversations and realisations
Learning to be thankful and how to take
responsibility for your own actions
All of those things are ordinary
He romanticised himself into an isolated misery
One that made him feel dead inside
Yes, experiencing the extraordinary is living
But the ordinary is what makes a life.

LIFE IS A FLAME

  Life is a little flame
Passed down from hand to hand
For you to hold for a time
And feel its warmth
The way its light flickers
Is what makes it perfect
and imperfect all at once
Burning within us until
We are extinguished
Back to the dust
Of what we were before.

NEED
EACH
OTHER

No single person
Can know everything
The world is a collection
Of dreams that have come
To reality
Over lifetimes

Passed down
Through generations
We need each other
And our collective conscious
To exist
Together

We are all
Little parts
Of the same organism
And each of us
In our own way
Contribute to the realisation
Of the universe
One experience at a time

All of them

Just as important as the last
The wonder of humanity
Is its need for beauty
To feel like it has really lived
For something more
Than being alive.

on work

Absurd

  The world is a play
And we are all performing
8 hours a day
5 days a week
Leaving only a little time
To be ourselves
But some people
Get lost in their characters.

freedom

Every now and then
On the way to work
I get a sudden surge of free will
And realise that I can do anything
I keep dreaming of playing hooky one day
Of taking a wrong turn
And continuing to walk
So, I can be unstuck for a day
And watch the world pass by
While I sit outside a café with a coffee
And drink it in my own time.

Begrudgingly

 More often than not
I wake up in the morning and groan
Sitting on the bus to work
Wishing I were back at home
I fill my time with distractions
Scroll through videos on my phone
To numb me from the thought
That in a city full of people, I am alone

Collectively working towards something
I couldn't tell you what
Watching life pass by
Reminded of all the things that you are not
Do you ever stop and ask yourself
What am I really doing this for?
This ceaseless rush for progression
Hurdling towards more things we can't afford
Bought with borrowed money
To keep us bound in a loop
Falling into bad habits
Just to see the week through

So many people
Are struggling every day just to get by
As we push ever forward
Without ever knowing why
Where are we going?

And why are we rushing so?
Distracted by the videos
Fed to us by our phones

Before I realise
Time and time again
That I should be grateful
To have my family and friends
A steady job
And a safe home
So much unhappiness
Comes from staring at a phone
Watching all the pixels
That tell you you're not enough
Until we disregard
The blessings that have been given to us
The little things
That are present in every day
The biggest challenge in life
Is to appreciate
The work.

10 years a tradie

   You get a glimpse into so many worlds as a tradie
Driving around the city from job to job
Houses, factories, office buildings, apartments
Living life like a fly on the wall
I've worked in houses
That have underground carparks that never end
And I've worked in council flats
That I hope I never see the inside of again

It forces you to witness
How some people really live
Let down by a system
That doesn't seem to give a shit
But some people have it so bad
It's like they never stood a chance at all
There's grime in the carpet
Black mould creeping up the walls
The TV plays
While cockroach-covered dishes sit in the sink
And even though their lives are devastating
They always chat and offer you a drink

I've worked in houses
Where the people in it are so rich
That staff will usher you out when the homeowners arrive
Because they hate to know that you exist
It makes me wonder

What money is really worth
When people can be miserable in mansions
And content in grime and dirt.

morning

Night turns to day
With the rising sun
That wakes up the world
With the music of birds
I put my headphones on
And wait in line for the bus
Before I work all day
The sky is blue outside
And I wish silently that I could be
Out beyond.

evening

When the day is done
I put my headphones on
Before I get the bus
And watch as the sun dips behind the horizon
But soon, all I can see is my own reflection
In the rattling window
Staring back in the darkness
I wonder where all the days go.

Dumb c*nts

  Older boys on site
Call the younger one's dumb cunts
And laugh at them when they wear
safety glasses and a mask
Older boys on site
Call the younger one's dumb cunts
Tell them they'll be right even after
they've breathed in asbestos dust

Dumb cunts
You know the invincible ones?
Same ones who refuse to check their lungs
Dumb cunts
The older ones that mould the younger ones
Pressure them to risk it all just to get a job done
Cover themselves in chemicals, work on live power
Powdered in dust like a baker covered in flour

Trust me, I did the same
And as I get older, I wonder if I'm destined
for an early grave
Just because I wanted
to save face
Risked my health just to get paid
For what? A couple hundred bucks a week?
Take a proper look at the industry and you'll see
It's full of dumb cunts like you and me

Who got fooled by the older boys with an entitlement
to mistreat
The younger ones who were just trying to be
A part of that tradie comradery
Who from an early age get a chip
knocked off their shoulder,
That they only start to see when they get older
And the damage is done.

Dumb cunts...

Brotherhood

  You'll never understand someone better
Then the guy you spend hours a day in a van with
Driving around the city from job to job
When I first started my apprenticeship
I knew my tradesman so well
That I could distinguish between all his different laughs
And decipher what kind of mood he was in
So, I could prepare for what kind of day I was about to have

I knew everything about him
All the good and the bad
Even all the small things
When you spend so much time with people
You get good at talking about nothing
Making funny stories out of the smallest moments
Doing jobs that make you question your life

Like crawling under houses
Over spiders' webs and dead rats
The only thing you can do is laugh sometimes
There's a sadistic kind of humour in the trades
That comes from putting your body on the line
Laughing so hard
Even in the times when we should have cried.

Polite drug dealer

  I sold weed for a couple of weeks
Before I quickly realised that it wasn't for me
Fast money always comes with a heavy price
But to be honest with you the problem
was that I'm way too nice
I didn't have the edge to be a dealer
I'm a lover, a laugher and a dreamer
And when someone bought a 2 for the night
I'd give them a 3 or at least a 2.5
I would have run myself broke if I'd kept it up
Trying to prove something to myself, I don't know what

But it's something I like to look back at and laugh
Because the irony in the desperation to prove who we are
Is that we end up going against our very nature
And ignore the things about ourselves that should be savoured
In the hopes of fitting in or being respected
But all the while, our true selves are neglected

Admitting who you are is a lot easier than you think
And the moment you do, it's like the whole world lifts
And suddenly you feel lighter than before
Because you're not carrying around a mask anymore.

Zero is a number

  I was working in an engine room beneath a building at Euston station in London
He and I were working there together
While the machines groaned and laboured
We laughed and told each other stories about our lives
He was Algerian,
The way he spoke was simple and poetic
Crafted by
A past life of youthful anger and ignorance, that had found wisdom
In the scars he had created
Against the world and himself

At school, he was smart but hated the structure
And no one seemed to believe in him
So, he grew resentful
It all felt meaningless
When he took his final exam, he wrote nothing but his name
And some made up answers
And handed the paper to his teacher
Who looked at him scornfully
"Give me zero then…" he said
But his teacher shook his head

"Zero is a number... You are nothing..." his teacher
replied, smiling
He told me the story as if he were still
standing there with his paper

He said it changed his life
After that, he put effort into everything he did
He ended up becoming a physics professor
And then an electrician in London
He fell in love
And never left
He loved literature
I told him I was writing a book
And he told me that the most beautiful stories are
always the simplest
Things that everyone can understand
Require little language
But carry the most meaning

I ended up getting fired from that job
The recruiter stitched me up and told them I was an
engineer
I never got a chance to speak to him again
I wonder if he's still working under there
Thinking of that time when his teacher
Told him he was nothing.

The panic of minutes

  When you're locked into the daily routine
Of waking up and going to work
Every minute is accounted for
And after a while
You start to find yourself in the same place, at the same time each day doing the same thing
That ceaseless routine becomes a necessity for life
When you live in a big city where time is of the essence

But the routine that helps get you through the week
Can rob you of your free will if you're not careful
You stop looking around
Stop wondering and day dreaming
It's like your thoughts are clouded by minutes
And the endless panic of chasing them
That's only broken from time to time
For a moment
A moment between moments
When you remember
That you are alive
Something much more than seconds
Minutes and hours
A feeling that only you understand
And so, I'm trying to remind myself to stop
And to look around, and think and dream

So that I can forget about minutes for a little while
And focus on what's important.

If there are no people

there is no art.

Money problems

  He was a chef when I met him
I was 21, living in London
Writing while I washed dishes at a café
There were deep bags under his eyes
Beaten like a dead horse
You want them eggs scrambled or fried?
He still had the energy to make us laugh
Sweating buckets in the kitchen
Yelling and swearing
I can still hear the bells ringing
He dreamed of being a lead singer
But was terrible at singing
He played the guitar
But time was ticking

I was broke when I knew him
All I ate were cans of soup
He told me to quit complaining
He said money problems are the easiest struggles that
life can throw at you
You get it, and it goes
That's just how money works
There was another chef in the kitchen
Who, only a month before, placed his mum
in a hearse

He asked me which
problem I'd rather have

He couldn't get through an entire day
Without a few lines of coke
Before he'd be depressed
But after, he'd crack jokes
He got his girlfriend pregnant
It seemed like it was the end of it all
He had no savings
But he said he always did best
when backed against the wall

He always had trouble connecting
Opening himself up
When I left his girlfriend was thinking
 of leaving him too
We used to keep in touch
But one day he disappeared
I couldn't find him anywhere online
And I've never spoken to him since
I often think about that time
And what he used to say
He was right about a lot
I hope he sorted his life out
One day I'll tell him I never forgot
That he always wanted to be a singer.

DO SOMETHING YOU LOVE

Artificial Intelligence

If you think of art as a product
You are missing half of its value

Art is blood, sweat, tears, laughter, joy
and entirely human.

AI has turned art into slop
And we into pigs
Who eat from the trough.

on family

We are children

  Boys blame their fathers
Until they get older
And realise that their father is a boy too
And his father before him
The world is made of children
Raising children

Blinded by the smog of the future
Making the best decisions they know how
And praying for a good outcome
What else could we hope to do?

In a world
Where people love one another but
don't know how to love themselves
Who are measured by material success
And have no time
To even question whether they are happy

Within every man
There is a little boy
Waiting to be free
So that he can laugh again
And breathe.

grief

  I'll picture him there forever
Walking through the forest with his little dog
Through overgrowth and fields of flowers
Throwing a little ball in silence
Thinking of beautiful stories
Even after a lifetime of grief
The wonder in life
Is making something sweet from
sadness
The hearts string's
Play soft notes when no one else
is around
Washed away by tears that make you feel
like a child again.

Our greatest mistakes are lived out by our children.

SAFE

Memories of early childhood
Full of sounds and smells
Wind chimes and strawberries in the garden
A treasure trove of purity
Kept at the centre of your heart
Where it's safe
From the world.

Reflection in the mirror

　How many men
　Look in the mirror and see
The man their fathers told them to be
Strong, unwavering and undefeatable
Almost immortal and invincible
While still being gentle, merciful
and compassionate
I wonder if any reasonable man
feels like he is all those things
Unblemished and full of self-assurance
In a world mostly full of boys
Raising boys
To be men consumed by insecurity and grief.

You are an amalgamation of everyone you meet.

We steer blindly through life but sometimes we look into the rear-view mirror and realise we made the wrong turn.

DANCE

  Life is one continuous dance
Where we are moving to and fro
We are the antithesis of our own existence
Our parents build us up
Only so we can tear ourselves
down again and start anew
Dancing under the shadows of great webs
Spun by something far more powerful than us
Wherever you look, there are memories
Of people who are gone and will never
come back
The taste is bittersweet
You can see them dancing there
Happy and free
Without you
And in time, you come to understand
That life is a solo dance.

FORGIVE YOURSELF

   Growing up is an act of forgiveness
For when we were young
And ignorant to the sacrifices of our parents
Who smiled at us even when they felt broken
Who we treated ungratefully in our tempers
Even sometimes hatefully as teenagers
Only to be loved in return
Parents who sacrificed it all
Without us ever even knowing
What it took for us to have a childhood
that felt happy and carefree.

Lost, Together

   You are directly connected
To three generations of stories before you
Your parents, their parents, and their parents
So many lifetimes of memory
That get passed down to you
If you're willing to listen
And learn the history of your family
And its journey through generations
Repeating itself over and over again through time
We realise that we are all the same
Lost, together, through all of our lives
Bound by the love and light that guides us home.

RETRACING

When I returned
To the country
Where my mum was born
I walked around the streets
My grandad used to call home
And was reminded of him
Wherever I went
Connected forever
In life and death

Retracing the footprints
That were made before
Even when
They aren't here anymore

In our own way
We all must
Carve a path
And make a life
True to what we are

Lost and found
Again and again
In laughter and tears
The language of
Family and friends

By and by
We travel

Along lonely roads
Retracing the footsteps
That lead back home.

on sadness and pain

REFLECTION

Most days
I look at myself
in the mirror.
But some days
I can't.

LAUGHING WHILE CRYING

In moments of joy, we laugh
In moments of sadness, we cry
But when a moment is beautiful
We do both.

STOP AND LOOK

The world moves at the same speed as you
That's why you have to stop and look
Otherwise, you'll miss it all
And wonder why everything feels different than before
Focused on arriving, never staying
Always working, never playing
Missing the little things that move silently by
Wondering what they were once you're alone at night.

EMANCIPATION

Everything exists in harmony with the Earth
Even when an animal destroys something
It proves to help something else
The world is a living organism
Creating and destroying itself over and over again
In balance
But we have isolated ourselves from it all
We have twisted the natural order
And plunged the world into chaos
And now we are spiralling
We have never been so connected, and yet
disconnected
all at once
as the world is happening around us
without us
anymore.

UP
And
DOWN

High and low
Are two opposite states
That are one in the same

Out of balance

Allow yourself to feel both
Without letting yourself be
swept away

The natural course of life
Is up and down
But the trick is
Existing in the middle.

BUTTERFLY

Where do the butterflies go
When there is no sun?
What do they do when they're not
dancing in the light?
Two weeks to live
To experience the joy of flight
Of colours, of smells, of a soft
breeze and a blue sky
For two weeks
Before they die
It's no wonder
They spend their lives dancing.

ANGER

So many men
Try to mask their sadness with anger
Because they don't know how
to look inwards
And feel.

Narcissus

There was a pitter patter on the roof
Rain fell, splashing against the leaves of trees outside
Frogs sang around a pond
As a fog floated gently above its surface
A thin veil of memory
Of things that happened long ago
When we were young
And there was magic in the world

I see him sitting there
By the pond
Transfixed by a love of self so strong
It had long ago turned to hatred
Into sorrow and grief
Of what he should have been

Lost in his own reflection
That shows him how it was before
I try to pull him away
But he doesn't notice me there anymore
There's a wall between us
One that can't be seen
But felt
I leave without looking back
And now whenever I hear the rain against my roof
I think of him
And wonder if the droplets

ever distorted his reflection
Would it make him see himself truly?
And the world around him
For what they are
I hope
When it does
He'll look up.

FLOWER

   When you die, do you float above your body?
You see it lying there and wonder
If it was ever really you at all
You try to look at yourself in the mirror
Nothing but a gentle waft of air and some specs of dust
Caught in a pillar of light seeping through the window
Soaring across the world, you travel far and wide
Only to find yourself back where you started
A flower is growing on your grave.

Feel, Together

The wonder of our species
Is our ability to make something
beautiful
From pain
To share with the world
So that we may feel
Together.

PAIN IS CONTAGIOUS

  Pain is contagious
We receive it and pass it on
One of my earliest memories
Was when I was 9 years old
Being bullied by the older boys on the bus
Because they said I looked like a girl
I wanted to know how it felt
To laugh at someone else
So, one afternoon, on the ride home
I saw another boy sitting at the bus stop by himself

He must have felt me looking
Because a moment later, he looked up
I took my chance
And laughed at him noiselessly behind the glass
I can still see the way his head dropped
Hurt and alone
I realised suddenly
How easy it is
To inflict your pain upon the world

And if there is a way
To break the cycle
Of all the hurt that gets passed on

It would start with forgiveness
For others, but also yourself
So that we can understand one another
With empathy and love.

ARTISTS/STARVING

I AM NOTHING
NOTHING, NOTHING, NOTHING
Something...
I AM EVERYTHING!
No, not everything...
Just a part of everything
Can't you see me burning?
Can you see my light?
It's all for you
I drown in the night

Performing
Even when no one can see
That's how I like it
You pass me on the street
Without realising
That I'm there
A shadow on the wall
That slips away when you stare

My invisibility is freedom
Unshackled by your eyes
That see right through
My dreams alight
Can't you see them burning for you?

My ego is hungry
Always wanting more
As I burn to ashes
What I was before
Can't you see the light?

PAIN

  The sweetest notes of life
Play when you are in pain
Watching little rivers run down
the window when it rains

Drinking in the sunset
Alone, but with the world
You have never been so aware
Of your place in it all.

COME, AND GO

  Flowers bloom
And wilt
People come
And go
Every moment is fourteen billion years
In the making
All of them have the same purpose
Of coming and going.

SONG

　Looking into the darkness
Engulfed in silence
Everything that is in you shows itself
Like a private cinema
Of old smells, and sounds
Play like a broken record
And from the darkness you hear
That song you made when you were a kid
Deep down you know you remember it.

on love

When I was 12, I had the sudden realisation that in a very short time, I would never be a kid again. I tried in vain to stop myself from growing. I slept curled up in a tight ball and wore shoes that were too small in hopes that they would slow the growth, but nothing worked. The night before my 13th birthday, I promised myself that I would never grow up. A promise that I kept close to my heart, even though I inevitably did. Inside all of us, there is a lost child that we must find again and keep safe from the world. We can turn to them when times are dark and heavy. When life feels like it's starting to fly by. The trap that we fall into as adults is that we focus too heavily on the bigger picture and forget to appreciate the little fabrics that sew it all. The child within you will help whenever you need it, because they see wonder in all things. They can show us how to live a better and simpler life, because they live closest to the heart, drawn by its light and warmth. Our duty as adults is to protect the child we have inside, and honour the promises that we made all those years ago, so that beyond the search for success and stability, we can find love and joy.

SELF SABOTAGE

  Whenever you're happy
You feel like you're teetering on the edge
So, you trip yourself on purpose
Because deep down you're scared
When you're feeling high
It suddenly dawns on you
That it can all be taken away
You trick yourself into believing
That after happiness, comes pain

Both these feelings are temporary
Happiness could never be a permanent state
The balance of your existence is you
Regardless of the way
You feel at the time
Let yourself feel it all
Know it, welcome it, and try to understand it
So that you never fall

Keep yourself even
Have empathy for who you are
Take it as it comes
Don't bottle it up
Or pretend it doesn't exist
Face it head on
Even though you may trip
We are human
And limited by our being

Worthy of self-love
Regardless of how you're feeling.

Get back up.

Melting into crowds

  Goodbyes are never how you imagine
You watch them melt into the crowd
Full of people just like you
Everything and nothing at all
Indistinguishable
But living and experiencing poetry in motion
In every moment
We are all just faces passing by
Going somewhere and nowhere at all
The movement of life
Is in the feeling of melting into crowds
Full of people just like you
Going somewhere and nowhere
All at once.

boys and girls

While teenage girls are watching romantic comedies
Teenage boys are watching porn
It's no wonder there are unrealistic expectations
On both sides
Of what a man and a woman really are.

BAD ADVICE

"Just fuck as many of them while you
still can"
Is what the older boys on site would tell me
That, and also, "never get married"
It made me wonder why anyone ever bothered with
love
Then I fell into it, got my heart broken
and figured one time was enough

Sometimes I watch movies and can't help but start
daydreaming
Asking myself if love as we know it is real or if it's just a
made-up feeling
Something to draw suckers in just for them to buy shit
Gain it, lose it again, then deny it

But now and then, I see a glimmer in someone's eye
When two people in love look at each other and can't
help but smile
And I know deep down that love is somewhere out
there for me
Maybe love is more than just a person, I'll have to wait
and see

Love is life, and the journey of understanding it
Love is not a currency
There's no way of owning it or commanding it

It's a surrender and an acceptance of a force much greater than you
And maybe in each person you love, you get a little closer to
Understanding yourself and what love is all for

Time after time
Even after marriage and divorce
For some reason, we still want to love
And that's what makes it so powerful.

FIGHT

Love is a battle
Until you surrender your heart
Joy and happiness, too
Until you surrender your laugh
Let go
Allow yourself to be swept away
Surrender yourself to life
To happiness and pain
What makes life beautiful
A story worth remembering in the end
Once you surrender to and cherish
What may never be again.

The loneliest person in the world is surrounded by the wrong people.

YOU ARE BEAUTIFUL

Why do we numb ourselves
Before learning how to love ourselves?
We are born crying
The journey of life is learning how
to laugh
At everything we are
Just people
Full of regrets and hopes
Success and failures
People just like those before us
Who use substance to cope
To bend and skew
The honest truth
That you are you
And that you are beautiful
Even though we are all just people
Full of insecurities and doubts
Sometimes it takes a whole lifetime
Just for us to see.

We wander far and wide, lost and trying to find somewhere we don't know yet. Every moment that passes is already in the past by the time you consider it. Few feelings are truly experienced in the present. Sex is one of them. Laughing and crying too. And surfing. The feeling of gliding down a wave, when all you can hear is wind rushing past your ears.

The first grief in life is the realisation that we'll never be children again. Like looking through a pane of glass, you can see your memories there, untouchable, on constant replay like a movie reel in an abandoned cinema. We meet people in life and wander with them for a time. They teach us different ways of looking at life. Different ways to approach and judge the world. Sometimes we grow, and sometimes we shrink into ourselves a little bit more. Like a flower folded in on itself from the night, opening and closing with the sun.

What was it all for?

TAKE THINGS AS THEY ARE, NOT WHAT YOU WANT THEM TO BE

My idea of love was formed by scenes I saw in movies
I treated each moment as though it were meant to be moving
Something deeply emotional that had to be of significance
The most beautiful realisation of my life was that it isn't.

BE FREE

Most moments arrive as they are
They aren't grand, they aren't beautiful, they aren't art
They come and go as they please
And all we could ever hope to be
Is grateful for each one that passes us by
And place in them your own meanings for life
So that you can guide yourself when it's dark
And go at the pace of your own beating heart.

**You are more
than a man or a woman**

  We all have pressures to live up to a certain expectation
Of what it means to be a man, or woman
And in the face of those expectations
We often fall short
In our own ways
Love yourself regardless
Even though it might take a lifetime
Just to learn how to

Be patient and understanding
Towards yourself
And other people too
Who are more than likely
Feeling just like you
And recognise that you are not complete
Because more than a man
Or a woman
You are human
And by nature
Full of imperfections
That make life
Beautiful and full of meaning
There is a reason
That you are you

Don't let those expectations
Rob the joy
Of being alive for the first time
And learning everything as you go
Making mistakes along the way
Realising after years that maybe you were wrong
Accepting things that you have always known were true deep down
But didn't want to say anything for fear of how it would make you feel
How it might make you reconsider
And love the world
And yourself too.

Here, together

  The wind rolls like waves through the grass
It sways gently back and forth with every breath
I am walking forward
Wherever I go
Because time only moves one direction
Until I close my eyes at night
And dream of the places I was before
Of the people I knew who aren't here anymore
I still feel their touch on my skin

I dream of places I have walked through
Of their sounds and smells
Strangers I've passed on the street
Different but just like me
Alive at this very moment
Out of all the moments that have ever been
We are all here in this one together
And that must count for something

So, while I'm here
For this short time
I will try to love and learn
to be loved just the same
Because I am alive in this very moment
Just like you
Together with the world
It must count for something.

The world is an oyster

But somebody has stolen all the pearls.

**NEVER BE AFRAID
TO CHASE A DREAM**

If you have a dream, you should chase it
Or at the very least, understand it
Let it root itself in who you are
And grow it slowly and deliberately
So that you can honour it
With years of servitude
To something far greater than you

An idea, a gift, a blessing and a curse
To have a dream is to live life in its fullest sense
Success and failure
Neither matters much
Because all things that happen
serve only to deepen your dreams
Richer and more beautiful

Never equate your success
With external judgment
You will lose your voice in the echo of
 other people's expectations
Instead, measure your dreams against yourself
Your understanding of who you are and your place in the world
The easiest way to drown a dream
Is to throw it into a sea of critics

Who understand little but have lots to say
And if you take their judgments too seriously
You'll lose your way
Only to find it again eventually
It is never too late
To live a dream
Honour yours, protect it
And never be afraid.

THE WALL

  Here I am at the wall
I've never been so close before
Banging against the stone and brick
Wondering if I'll ever get in
It makes me wonder
And makes me think
Will it all be worth it?
All the years of chasing this dream
Never really understanding what it means
Blundering blindly in the dark
Feeling close yet still so far
I steady myself and get ready to push
And remind myself of all the work it took
Just to be stood here at the edge of the wall
Thankful that I'm here with you all
I'm never going to stop pushing
Until we're all in.

CHASE

I'll never stop chasing this dream
Even after I succeed
I think back to when it first started
I was seventeen, sleeping under a table
at my brother's uni share house
Reading and writing every night
At first, it was just a way to make sense of life
Before I realised that it could give me the drive to change mine

From young I was always working
Everything I've ever done, I've had to earn it
Working 2-3 jobs at once
Sleeping 3-4 hours a night
Saving up to move to London
Chasing the dream to write
Only to have it crushed by the weight of a big city
I was 22 when I came back
Broker than ever and full of self-pity

On the tools and learning to survive
Writing things that I knew would never see the light
Until I bought a typewriter one day and started a stall
And that one small decision changed it all
Because suddenly there were people who began to support

And I didn't feel alone like I did before
I wrote books and tried to get them into every store in the city
But I was young and more often than not they wanted nothing to do with me

So, I started leaving my books on their shelves anyway
I started leaving them everywhere, everyday
People's mailboxes, supermarket shelves, building sites, bus seats
Hoping that one day someone would get back to me
The road to your dreams is a dense fog
Work your way through and never stop
So, I'm still pushing and doing everything I can
And all I hope is that you understand
That I'm grateful for it all
And for all the people I've met along the way.

Thank you for the support.

Live True

I was waiting for you
You say to yourself
When you finally live true
Always watching
Waiting patient
To realise you have nothing to prove
Live your life how you see fit
Do it with love and grace
With empathy and passion
And for the love of God, be brave
Do the things that make you scared
No one will ever truly care
So, live like no one is watching.

The End

Thank you for reading this book. I wrote a lot of these poems a few years ago, but left them for some time while I travelled and tried to figure out my life a little bit. A little bit turned into a little longer, and then I distanced myself from poetry almost entirely while I worked on YOUTH. A few months after I released YOUTH, and the dust of it all was settled, I was going through my computer one day when I found the file that contained all of the old poems I'd been working on, and so I picked up where I left off.
It was a lot of fun, going through these poems, removing some and adding more, and in a way, it solidified them for me, because I still agreed with most of them even years later.
I hope that you found something in them, and if you like my work, please check out my other stuff on my Instagram @poemboii, or my website www.poemboii.com.

Thanks for all the support

E.S. Higgins
(poemboii)

ABOUT THE AUTHOR

Evered Higgins is a writer and poet from the Northern Beaches of Sydney. In the early stages of his writing journey, while he was midway through an electrical apprenticeship, he bought a used typewriter and started writing on the spot poetry at the Manly Markets. While best known for poetry, he also writes fiction, and released his debut novel YOUTH in 2025.

If you like Evered's work, you can find him on his Instagram @poemboii, or on his website.

www.poemboii.com

www.ingramcontent.com/pod-product-compliance
Lightning Source LLC
LaVergne TN
LVHW092053060526
838201LV00047B/1378